Cakes
& Bakes

Sphere
First published in Great Britain in 2016 by Sphere

ISBN 978-0-7515-6634-5

Printed in Italy

Book creation and design by Harris + Wilson Ltd
Cakes created by Bath Cake Company

Art Director: Manisha Patel
Managing Editor: Judy Barratt
Photographer: Emily Dennison
Recipe writer and editor: Nicola Graimes

10 9 8 7 6 5 4 3 2 1

Papers used by Sphere are from well-managed forests and other responsible sources

MIX
Paper from
responsible sources
FSC® C104740

A CIP catalogue record for this book is available from the British Library.

Sphere
An imprint of
Little, Brown Book Group, Carmelite House,
50 Victoria Embankment, London EC4Y 0DZ
An Hachette UK Company
www.hachette.co.uk
www.littlebrown.co.uk

Cakes
& Bakes

Sweet! Tasty! Delicious!

Recipes from the Candy Kingdom

sphere

Contents

Delicious!

Getting started

Our first Cakes & Bakes book is just like Candy Crush Saga itself – easy to start and fun to do. Throughout the book, you'll find cakes and treats that make your mouth water and leave you wanting to savour just one more bite... Divine!

All you really need to get started on your sweet baking adventure are a few fundamental cake ingredients – butter, sugar, eggs, milk, icing sugar – and some basic sugarcraft tools. We've listed the tools in the handy box, opposite, so that you can tick them off as you gather them.

TASTY! BASIC CAKES AND COOKIES

On pages 8–11 you'll find the recipes for the basic vanilla sponge cake and vanilla cupcakes (along with flavour variations), shortbread biscuits and gingerbread cookies, which come up throughout the book. We recommend you read the instructions relating to the specific cakes and bakes before you start, just in case there are any variations it's best to consider at the outset.

SWEET! ALL THE FROSTING YOU NEED

To make the Candy Kingdom cakes and bakes as sweet as they can be, you'll need frosting: on pages 12–13, you'll find the recipes for perfect buttercream and smooth royal icing, and a delicious recipe for chocolate ganache that we know would make chocoholic Yeti very happy!

Decorating tools

Large serrated knife
Palette knife
Cake smoother
Metal cake side smoother
Edible glue
Paint brush
Pastry brush
Rolling pin
Wheel tool
Bone tool
Dresden tool
Ball tool
Cone tool
Cake board/drum

Cutters

10cm/4in star cutter
10cm/4in 5-petalled
flower cutter
2cm/¾in rose leaf cutter
5cm/2in round cutter
15cm/6in Candy cane
cutter
12cm/4½in fish cutter

Frosting tools

Piping bags
Disposable piping bags
#2 and #3 piping nozzles
Medium and large star
nozzles

CANDY KINGDOM CLOUDS

Each of the cakes and bakes has a Candy Kingdom cloud floating above it. The level in the cloud indicates the skill level for that particular treat – Level 1s are super-easy, Level 2s are more involved, and Level 3s have serious wow factor.

TIFFI'S TIPS

Look out for Tiffi's Tips. These give tips and shortcuts, or ways to adapt each treat for extra Candy sweetness.

CUT-OUT TEMPLATES

If you're wondering how you'll ever get your Swedish Fish cookies so perfect, look no further. Copy the templates on pages 106–111 for these and other Candy Kingdom shapes. Cut out the copies and place them over the dough or icing to cut around.

Tasty!

Vanilla Sponge Cake

For a 20cm/8in cake

- 175g/6oz softened butter, plus extra for greasing
- 175g/6oz self-raising flour, sifted, plus extra for dusting
- 175g/6oz caster sugar
- 3 eggs, lightly beaten
- 1 teaspoon vanilla extract

For a 23cm/9in cake

- 250g/9oz softened butter, plus extra for greasing
- 250g/9oz self-raising flour, sifted, plus extra for dusting
- 250g/9oz caster sugar
- 4 eggs, lightly beaten
- 1½ teaspoons vanilla extract

1 Preheat the oven to 180°C/360°F/Gas 4. Grease and flour the sides and line the base of a cake tin with baking paper. Whisk together the butter and sugar until pale and creamy. Whisk in the eggs, one at a time, scraping down the bowl after each addition, then whisk in the vanilla, until combined. Using a metal spoon, fold in the flour in two batches, until combined.

2 Spoon the batter into the prepared tin, level the top, and bake for 30–35 minutes or until a skewer inserted into the middle comes out clean. Leave to cool in the tin for 5 minutes, then transfer to a wire rack to cool completely.

FLAVOUR VARIATION

Chocolate: Replace 2–3 tablespoons of the flour with 2–3 tablespoons of unsweetened cocoa powder.

8

Vanilla Cupcakes

Makes 10

- 250g/9oz plain flour
- 2 teaspoons baking powder
- 175g/6oz golden caster sugar

- 125g/4½oz butter
- 2 large free-range eggs
- 2 teaspoons vanilla extract
- 200ml/7fl oz whole milk

Method

1 Preheat the oven to 200°C/400°F/Gas 6. Put 10 cupcake cases into a large muffin tin. Sift the flour, baking powder and sugar into a large mixing bowl, then stir with a wooden spoon.

2 Melt the butter in a pan, leave to cool slightly, then pour into a second mixing bowl. Whisk in the eggs, vanilla and milk. Pour the egg mixture into the dry ingredients and combine.

3 Spoon the batter into the paper cases until about two thirds full. Bake for 20-25 minutes until risen and light golden. Place the cakes on a wire rack to cool.

FLAVOUR VARIATIONS

Lemon: Stir in the finely grated zest of 1 unwaxed lemon and replace 2 tablespoons of the milk with lemon juice.
Chocolate: Replace 2 tablespoons of the flour with 2 tablespoons of unsweetened cocoa powder.

Gingerbread Biscuits

Makes about 8–10 biscuits

- 175g/6oz plain flour, plus extra for dusting
- 2 teaspoons ground ginger
- ½ teaspoon bicarbonate of soda
- 55g/2oz butter
- 85g/3oz dark muscovado sugar
- 2 tablespoons golden syrup
- 1 egg, lightly beaten

Method

1 Preheat the oven to 190°C/375°F/Gas 5. Line 2 large baking sheets with baking paper. Sift the flour, ginger and bicarbonate of soda into a large mixing bowl. Using your fingertips, rub in the butter until the mixture resembles fine breadcrumbs. Mix in the sugar.

2 Warm the golden syrup until liquid, leave to cool slightly, then add to the flour mixture with the egg. Stir with a fork to make a soft dough – if it is too sticky add a little extra flour and stir again.

3 Roll out the dough on a lightly floured work surface to 5mm/¼in thick. Using a cutter of choice, stamp out the biscuits, re-rolling the dough when necessary. Place on the prepared baking sheets and bake for 12–15 minutes until just crisp and golden. Leave to cool on a wire rack before decorating.

Shortbread Biscuits

Makes about 8-10 biscuits

- 165g/5¾oz plain flour, plus extra for dusting
- 55g/2oz caster sugar
- 115g/4oz butter

Method

1. Preheat the oven to 180°C/360°F/Gas 4. Line a baking sheet with baking paper. Sift the flour into a large mixing bowl, then stir in the sugar.

2. Rub in the butter with your fingertips, then press the mixture together to form a soft dough.

3. Place the dough between 2 sheets of cling film, then roll out until about 5mm/¼in thick. Peel away the top layer of cling film from the dough. Using a cutter of choice, stamp out the biscuits, re-rolling the dough when necessary. Carefully lift the biscuits from the lower layer of cling film and place them on the prepared baking sheet. Bake for 15-25 minutes (the amount of time will depend upon the size and shape of the biscuits) until pale golden. Leave to cool on a wire rack before decorating.

Buttercream Frosting

Makes enough to cover one 23cm/9in cake or 10 cupcakes

- 150g/5½oz softened butter
- 325g/11½oz icing sugar
- 2 teaspoons milk
- food-colouring paste, as necessary

Method

1 Whisk all the ingredients together using a hand-held mixer or food processor for 3–4 minutes until smooth and fluffy.

2 To colour your buttercream, add food colouring, a little at a time, stirring to combine between each addition, until you have reached the colour you need.

Royal Icing

Makes enough to decorate 10 biscuits (you can freeze any left over)

- 500g/1lb 2oz icing sugar
- 3½ tablespoons dried egg white

Tiffi's Tip
If you need to make coloured royal icing, simply mix in a little food-colouring paste.

Method

1 Combine the icing sugar and dried egg white in the bowl of a food processor. Using the beater attachment and with the motor running, add 6½ tablespoons water. Mix on a medium speed for 7–10 minutes, until the icing is smooth and glossy.

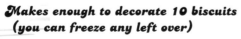

Tiffi's Tip

You'll need buttercream or royal icing for decorating, but don't forget the ready-to-roll fondant icing, too! There are loads of great colours you can buy from baking stores without having to make your own – simply unwrap, roll out and away you go!

Chocolate Ganache

Makes enough to cover one 23cm/9in cake

- 225ml/8fl oz double cream
- 250g/9oz plain chocolate
- 25g/1oz butter

Method

1 Pour the cream into a small saucepan and heat gently over a medium heat. Meanwhile, put the chocolate and butter into a heatproof mixing bowl. As soon as the cream starts to boil, remove it from the heat.

2 Pour the hot cream over the chocolate and butter and stir until the chocolate has melted and the ganache is glossy and smooth. Leave to firm up at room temperature.

Cakes
& Bakes

Level 1

Star Iced Cookies

We're opening our book with something deliciously tasty but super-simple. Award yourself all three stars for sweetness!

Makes 9

- 1 quantity Gingerbread Biscuits (see page 10)
- 100g/3½oz red ready-to-roll icing
- icing sugar or cornflour, for dusting
- 100g/3½oz green ready-to-roll icing
- 100g/3½oz yellow ready-to-roll icing

Method

1 Preheat the oven, prepare a baking sheet and make the gingerbread biscuit dough following steps 1 and 2 on page 10.

2 Roll out the dough to 5mm/¼in thick on a lightly floured work surface. Using a 10cm/4in star cutter, or the template on page 107, cut out 9 cookies, re-rolling the dough as necessary. Place the stars on the prepared baking sheet and bake for 12–15 minutes until just crisp and golden. Leave to cool.

3 Knead the red ready-to-roll icing until softened. Dust the work surface with icing sugar or cornflour and roll out the icing to 3mm/⅛in thick. Cut out three stars using the star-shaped cutter or template. Brush the cooled biscuits with edible glue and stick the red icing stars to three biscuits. Repeat with the green and yellow icing and the remaining gingerbread stars.

Leabharlanna Fhine Gall

Tiffi's Tip
To prevent the stars losing their shape as they cook, chill the cut dough for 30 minutes before baking.

To create the star shape use a star cutter or the template on page 107.

Level 2

Yeti Cake Surprise

Candy surprises are the best surprises in the Candy Kingdom. This cake has a fluffy, sugary coating and tasty Candies hidden in the middle. We think Yeti – the coolest guy in Candy Town – would be very proud of the cake that bears his name.

 Makes one 20cm/8in cake

- 3 x 20cm/8in Vanilla Sponge Cakes (see page 8)
- 1½ quantities Buttercream Frosting (see page 12)
- raspberry or strawberry jam, for spreading
- crisp sugar-coated chocolates or other sweets, for filling

Method

1 Make the cakes following the recipe instructions on page 8. Turn out the cakes from the tins and allow them to cool completely, then level the top of each cake with a large serrated knife.

2 Cut out a 12cm/4½in diameter hole from the centre of two of the cakes, so that you have two sponge 'rings' and one complete cake.

3 Set aside two thirds of the buttercream (you'll need this to cover the outside of the cake after you've constructed it). Halve the remaining buttercream.

4 Take one of the sponge rings and, using a palette knife, spread a layer of jam over the top of the ring. Wipe clean your palette knife and repeat with the buttercream so that you have a layer of jam topped with a layer of buttercream. Sandwich the two rings together.

5 Fill the cake cavity with sweets, so that the sweets come to the top of the hole, but not higher than it. You've just created Yeti's Candy surprise from within his special cake!

Tiffi's Tip #1
Don't throw away the cut-out piece of cake! Crumble it up, put the crumbs in freezer bags and freeze them for cake pops (see pages 82 and 102).

Tiffi's Tip #2
Ramp up the surprise factor when you cut the cake open by making your layers multi-coloured. Simply add a few drops of different food colourings to the sponge mixture before you bake the cakes!

6 Wipe clean your palette knife again and spread a second layer of jam over the uppermost sponge ring. Wipe the knife clean and spread over the remaining half of the buttercream. Now, top everything with the third, intact cake to conceal the hole in the centre.

7 Using a serrated knife, carefully carve the uppermost cake so that you create a dome shape. You don't have to be too precise because you can correct any dents or nicks with the buttercream topping. Shave away, bit by bit, until you're happy with your shape.

8 Use your palette knife to cover the whole cake in the reserved two thirds of buttercream in a nice, even layer. Fluff up the buttercream using the tip of a palette knife to create the effect of Yeti's fur. When you cut open the cake, all your Candies will cascade out in a special Yeti surprise. Delicious!

Gingerbread Girls

We love the big, smiley grins on these tasty Gingerbread Girl cookies. You'll need to gather a #3 nozzle and a piping bag for this baking project. It might take some practice to perfect the detail, but the results are divine!

Makes 8

- 1 quantity Gingerbread Biscuits (see page 10)
- 100g/3½oz white Royal Icing (see page 12)

- 20g/¾oz pale pink ready-to-roll icing
- 20g/¾oz green ready-to-roll icing

Method

1 Gather together the tools you'll need to decorate your Gingerbread Girls – a #3 nozzle, a piping bag, and some edible glue to do the sticking.

2 Preheat the oven, prepare a baking sheet and make the gingerbread biscuit dough following steps 1 and 2 on page 10, then roll out the dough to 5mm/¼in thick on a lightly floured work surface. Using a Gingerbread Girl cutter, or the template on page 110, cut out eight biscuits, re-rolling the dough as necessary.

Use a Gingerbread Girl cutter for the shape, or try the template on page 110.

3 When you have all your Gingerbread Girls, place the them on the prepared baking sheets and bake them at 180°C/360°F/ Gas 4 for 12-15 minutes until just crisp and golden – take care not to let them colour too much. Leave the biscuits to cool on a wire rack before decorating.

4 Fit the #3 nozzle to your piping bag and fill the bag with the white royal icing. This is the fun bit! Start decorating your Gingerbread Girls.... First, pipe in her arms – piping around the edge of each arm section and finishing the oval shape within the main body in one swift movement each time.

5 Now, pipe a white line around the outside edge of the rest of each biscuit, skipping over the lines you've made for the arms. You should now have the perfect outline of your Gingerbread Girls.

6 Then, for each biscuit, pipe in her hair (don't forget her bunches), eyebrows, eyes, nose, and big, smiley mouth. Finally, pipe a wavy line at the bottom of her dress.

7 Roll out 16 small balls of pink ready-to-roll icing to make all the buttons. Attach two pink balls to each dress, as in the picture, with edible glue. Repeat, making the balls slightly smaller, for the dots on the insides of her arms, at her 'shoulders'.

8 To make the eight hair bows, roll three balls of green icing per bow, flattening two a little for the outer parts of the bow. Construct the bow on each biscuit, attaching the pieces using edible glue. Roll two further balls of green icing per biscuit, to make the hairbands; attach using edible glue. Your Gingerbread Girls are accessorized with big smiles, and ready to begin their Candy Kingdom adventure!

Level 1

Peppermint Palace Cupcakes

Genie Jellybeanie invites you to Peppermint Palace for some divine pink buttercream treats, topped with peppermint!

 **Makes 10**

- 1 quantity Vanilla Cupcakes (see page 9)
- ⅛ teaspoon pink food-colouring paste

- 1 quantity Buttercream Frosting (see page 12)
- peppermint flavouring, to taste
- 10 striped peppermint sweets, to decorate

Method

1 Using brown cupcake cases, make the cupcakes following the instructions on page 9.

2 Stir the pink food-colouring paste into the buttercream until you have an even shade of pink. Add the peppermint flavouring 1 or 2 drops at a time, to taste.

3 Spoon the peppermint buttercream into a piping bag fitted with a large star nozzle. Pipe the buttercream, using a spiral motion, on the top of each cupcake in a large swirl. Top each cupcake with a peppermint sweet to finish. Easy!

Odus the Owl Cake

Once you're past level 50 in Candy Crush Saga you'll discover Dreamworld, where Tiffi goes as she sleeps. Friendly Odus the Owl carries her there. In our cake Odus is perfectly perched on his crescent moon – just as he should be during gameplay.

 Makes one 20cm/8in cake

- 2 x 20cm/8in Vanilla Sponge Cakes (see page 8)
- 1 quantity Buttercream Frosting (see page 12)
- 750g/1lb 10oz white ready-to-roll icing
- icing sugar or cornflour, for dusting
- 100g/3½oz purple ready-to-roll icing
- 10g/¼oz orange ready-to-roll icing
- gold lustre paint, for decorating
- 50g/1¾oz yellow ready-to-roll icing
- 20g/¾oz lilac ready-to-roll icing

Method

1 Make the cakes following the vanilla sponge recipe instructions on page 8. Remove from the tins, cool completely, then level the top of each cake with a large serrated knife.

2 Using a palette knife, spread about one third of the buttercream frosting over the top of one cake and sandwich the two cakes together.

3 Secure the cake to a 25cm/10in cake board or drum with a small amount of buttercream. Using a palette knife, spread the remaining buttercream over the top and down the sides of the whole cake in a smooth, even layer.

4 Knead the white ready-to-roll icing until soft and pliable. Dust a work surface with icing sugar or cornflour and roll out the white icing into a circle large enough to cover the cake and the board, and so that it is about 5mm/¼in thick.

5 Using a rolling pin, lift the icing and drape it over the top of the cake and board. Smooth it down using a cake smoother, starting on the top, then working down the sides and the board to remove any trapped air or creases. Trim the edge of the icing using a small knife and reserve the offcuts. Decorate the edge of the board and the bottom of the cake with a yellow ribbon, using edible glue to secure into place.

6 Mix some of the purple icing with a little of the leftover white, kneading it together in your hands until you have a uniform colour that is a lighter shade of purple for Odus's body.

7 Dust the work surface with icing sugar or cornflour and roll out the lighter and darker shades of purple icing to about 3mm/⅛in thick. Using the templates on page 111, cut out the head and wings from the darker purple, and the body from the lighter. Arrange them all on the cake, attaching them with edible glue. To make the 'ears', roll a thin sausage of purple icing, then roll out some white and cut it into short, thin strips (you'll need about 10). Wrap the white strips around the purple roll, spacing them evenly. Cut the ears to length and stick to the cake.

8 To make the eyes, cut out two ovals of white icing (see template) and two circles of purple (for the pupils) and attach them to Odus, as in the picture, with edible glue. Brush two small rounds of white icing with gold paint, then attach these at the top of his wings where they join his body.

9 To make the moon, roll out the yellow icing to 3mm/⅛in thick. Cut out a moon shape (again using the template on page 111) and attach this to the cake with edible glue, too, leaving enough space to attach his claws so that they will sit on the lilac edging. To make the edging, roll a long sausage of lilac icing and stick it around the edge of the moon with edible glue. Shape the orange icing into a little beak and six claws (three for each foot) and attach them with edible glue. Hey presto! Odus is ready to watch over Tiffi and her Dreamworld adventures!

To create Odus and the moon shape, use the templates on page 111.

Easter Egg Biscuits

All over the Easter Bunny Hills lie sweet and delicious Easter eggs nestled in the grass – these iced biscuits are decorated to look just like them. You'll need #2 nozzles and eight piping bags to be able to do the decorating – time to get creative with the frosting tools!

Makes 9

- 1 quantity Shortbread Biscuits (see page 11)
- 50g/1¾oz yellow Royal Icing (see page 12)
- 50g/1¾oz light blue Royal Icing
- 50g/1¾oz dark blue Royal Icing
- 50g/1¾oz pink Royal Icing
- 50g/1¾oz white Royal Icing

Method

1 Preheat the oven, prepare a baking sheet and make the shortbread biscuit dough following steps 1 and 2 on page 11. Roll out the dough between two sheets of cling film to about 5mm/¼in thick. Peel away the top layer of cling film and, using a 10cm/4in egg-shaped cutter, or the template on page 109, cut out 9 biscuits from the dough, re-rolling as necessary.

2 Place the egg-shaped biscuits on the prepared baking sheets and bake for 15–20 minutes until pale golden. Leave the cookies to cool on a wire rack before decorating. Meanwhile, gather three #2 nozzles and eight disposable piping bags.

3 Fit three of the piping bags with a nozzle and fill one with a third of the yellow icing, one with a third of the light blue icing, and one with a third of the dark blue icing.

To create the eggs use an egg-shaped cutter or the template on page 109.

4 Pipe a yellow line around the outside edge of three of the biscuits, then repeat with the light

blue icing on a further three biscuits. Pipe a dark blue line around the outside edge of the remaining biscuits, with a dark blue zig-zag line across the top, so that these eggs look as though they have a cracked shell.

5 Add a little water to the remaining coloured icing (including the pink and also the white) until each colour has the consistency of single cream. Fill the remaining piping bags each with a different colour, then snip off the ends so that each one has a hole about 3mm/⅛in wide.

6 Pipe the yellow icing within the yellow borders, gently pushing it out to the border line, then repeat with the light blue icing in the light blue borders. Fill the lower (larger) portion of the dark blue eggs with dark blue icing and fill the top section of the dark blue eggs with pink icing.

7 Using the white icing piping bag, pipe small white dots onto the light blue and the yellow eggs while the bases are still wet. Leave all the biscuits to dry before you tuck in.

Tiffi's Iced Candy Cupcakes

Our Cakes & Bakes book wouldn't be complete without a treat specially made for Tiffi. We think she would love these swirly iced cupcakes topped with her favourite Candies in the brightest colours. Delicious!

Makes 10

- 1 quantity Vanilla Cupcakes (see page 9)

- 1 quantity Buttercream Frosting (see page 12)
- jelly beans, to decorate

Method

1 Make the cupcakes, using brightly coloured cupcake cases, following the instructions on page 9. Leave the cupcakes to cool on a wire rack before you begin to decorate.

2 While the cupcakes are cooling, make the buttercream frosting using the instructions on page 12. We've kept our frosting plain for Tiffi's cakes, but you can colour it if you like.

3 Spoon the buttercream into a piping bag fitted with a large star nozzle. Pipe the buttercream, using a spiral motion, on the top of each cupcake in a large swirl. Decorate the cupcakes with jelly beans. Sweet!

Tiffi's Tip
Make sure the
buttercream is
soft before you pipe.

Booster Wheel Cake

Spin the Booster Wheel for your daily Candy! If you fill the segments in your cake with all your favourite sweets, you're guaranteed a delectable treat with every slice! We've chosen the most colourful Candies we could find – but you can use any that you feel will take you right to the heart of the Candy Kingdom.

Makes one 20cm/8in cake

- 2 x 20cm/8in Vanilla Sponge Cakes (see page 8)
- 200g/7oz white ready-to-roll icing
- icing sugar or cornflour, for dusting
- 1 quantity Buttercream Icing (see page 12) or Chocolate Ganache (see page 13)
- 4 x 114g/4oz packs chocolate fingers, about 75 biscuits in total
- your favourite sweets, such as jelly beans, Candy-coated chocolates, marshmallows, dolly mixtures, chocolate drops and wine gums
- 50g/1¾oz pink ready-to-roll icing

Method

1 Make the cakes following the recipe on page 8. Remove from the tins, cool completely, then level the top of each cake using a large serrated knife. While the cakes are cooling, lightly brush a 28cm/11in cake board or drum with water.

2 Knead the white ready-to-roll icing until softened. Dust a work surface with icing sugar or cornflour and roll out the icing until large enough to cover the cake board, about 5mm/¼in

thick. Lay the icing on the board, smooth with a cake smoother, and trim the edges with a small knife. Set aside.

3 Using a palette knife, spread about one-third of the ganache or buttercream over the top of one cake and sandwich the two cakes together. Dot the board with a small amount of ganache or buttercream.

4 Secure the cake to the cake board using the dotted ganache or buttercream as glue. Spread the remaining ganache or buttercream over the top and down the sides of the cake in a smooth, even layer.

5 Press the chocolate fingers upright around the cake edge, reserving eight to decorate the top – make sure they sit just above the top edge of the cake to stop the sweets falling off.

6 Arrange the reserved chocolate fingers on the top of the cake to create eight equally sized segments. Fill each segment with one type of your favourite sweets to create a colourful Booster Wheel effect.

7 Roll the pink ready-to-roll icing into a ball, flatten the top a little, and place it in the middle of the cake to form the centre of the chocolate-finger spokes. Attach a ribbon around the bottom of the cake and fix the loose ends using a small amount of chocolate ganache or buttercream.

Level 1

Lollipop Forest Flower Cookies

These delicious flower-shaped cookies sandwiched with sweet buttercream are inspired by the flowers that grow throughout the Lollipop Forest. We couldn't resist recreating them for our Cakes & Bakes book. We've used fondant icing for the centre of each flower to keep things simple, but (if you were feeling really sweet) you could cut a hole in half the cookies before you bake them, then when they're cooled and sandwiched together fill the centre with strawberry jam instead.

Makes 10

- 2 quantities Shortbread Biscuits (see page 11)
- ⅓ quantity Buttercream Frosting (see page 12)

- 50g/1¾oz red read-to-roll icing
- icing sugar or cornflour, for dusting

Method

1 Preheat the oven and make double the quantity of shortbread biscuit dough following the instructions on page 11. Remember to prepare two baking trays by lining them with baking paper, rather than just one.

2 Place the dough between 2 sheets of cling film (you may have to do this in two parts as you have twice as much dough), then roll out until about 5mm/¼in thick. Remove the top layer of cling film and, using a 10cm/4in flower-shaped cutter, or the template on page 108, cut out 20 cookies, re-rolling the dough when necessary.

3 Place the flowers on the prepared baking sheets. If you want to mark out the petals, as shown, use the edge of a palette knife to demarcate each petal edge, before baking. Then, bake the biscuits in the preheated oven for 15–20 minutes until pale golden. Leave to cool on a wire rack before decorating.

To create the flower shape, use a standard 5-petalled cookie cutter or the template on page 108.

Tiffi's Tip

If you want to make these cookies extra-divine, try sandwiching them together with not only buttercream, but strawberry jam, too!

4 Once the biscuits are cool, sandwich the shortbread flowers together with a layer of buttercream, so that you have 10 sandwiched cookies.

5 Knead the red ready-to-roll icing until softened. Dust a work surface with icing sugar or cornflour and roll out the icing until it is 3mm/⅛in thick. Cut out 10 red circles using a 2cm/¾in round cutter. Brush the middle of each biscuit with edible glue and stick a red circle on top. Divine!

Level 2

Four-layered Frosting Blocker Cakes

The Four-layered Frosting Blockers can be tricky to break down in the Candy Crush Saga, needing four hits before they'll disappear. We're confident these delicious individual cakes won't be so stubborn! With their layers of divine buttercream frosting, they'll be gone in just one... .

Makes 4

- 1 quantity 20cm/8in Vanilla Sponge Cake batter (see page 8)
- ½ quantity Buttercream Frosting (see page 12)

- red food-colouring paste, to decorate
- 50g/1¾oz plain chocolate, broken into pieces

Method

1 Grease and flour the sides and line the base of a 15cm/6in square cake tin. Preheat the oven and make the cake batter (there's no need to reduce the batter quantity, as you want your Blocker cakes to be nice and deep) following step 1 of the instructions on page 8.

2 Spoon the batter into the prepared tin, level the top and bake for 35–40 minutes, or until a skewer inserted into the centre comes out clean and the top is golden. Remove the cake from the tin, and leave on a wire rack to cool completely.

3 Once the cake is cool, level the top with a large serrated knife. Transfer the cake to a board or other flat surface and cut it into quarters.

4 Using a palette knife, spread half the buttercream over the top of each cake in an even layer. Try to make it as smooth as you can. Gather together three piping bags in order to finish decorating the cakes.

5 Colour two thirds of the remaining buttercream with the red food-colouring paste until you have an even, vibrant red colour. Then, spoon the red buttercream into a piping bag fitted with a large star nozzle. Using a spiral motion, pipe the red buttercream on the top of each cake in a large swirl. Leave enough room around the edges of the cake to pipe in the

Tiffi's Tip #1
Try making Two-layered and Three-layered Blockers, too, to complete the Candy Crush Frosting Blocker family!

Tiffi's Tip #2

These Blockers make brilliant traybake cakes, too. Make a larger, square sponge and, once cooled, cut up the cake into smaller squares, then decorate to scale.

chocolate wavy lines later. Flatten the top of each red swirl a little, ready to receive the next layer in the Blocker.

6 Spoon the remaining plain buttercream into a separate piping bag fitted with a medium star nozzle. Pipe a slightly smaller plain-coloured swirl on top of the red buttercream swirl.

7 Gently melt the chocolate in a microwave (or in a bowl over a pan of simmering water, if you don't have a microwave), then spoon it into the final piping bag. Snip a small hole at the end of the bag, about 2mm/1⁄16in wide, and pipe a zigzag pattern around the edge of each cake. That's it! Your Blockers are ready. Tuck in!

Four-layered Frosting Blocker Cakes

Denize the Dragon Cake

Emerging from the Lemonade Lake is the Candy Kingdom's very own friendly dragon, Denize. You'll need to do some super sugarcraft for this creation, so give yourself plenty of time.

Makes one 23cm/9in cake

- 2 x 23cm/9in Vanilla Sponge Cakes (see page 8)
- 1½ quantities Buttercream Frosting (see page 12)
- 950g/2lb 2oz white ready-to-roll icing
- 150g/5½oz brown ready-to-roll icing
- 50g/1¾oz yellow ready-to-roll icing
- 50g/1¾oz green ready-to-roll icing
- 50g/1¾oz red ready-to-roll icing

FOR THE DRAGON
- 200g/7oz bright pink modelling paste
- icing sugar or cornflour, for dusting
- 10g/¼oz black modelling paste
- 10g/¼oz white modelling paste

FOR THE LOLLIPOPS
- 50g/1¾oz red modelling paste
- 50g/1¾oz green modelling paste
- 50g/1¾oz yellow modelling paste

Tiffi's Tip
The day before you plan to bake and decorate the cake, make the dragon and lollipop features as they need at least 24 hours to dry and firm up.

TO MAKE THE DRAGON

1 Knead the pink modelling paste until softened. Using your hands, shape two thirds of the paste into the dragon's head and neck, using a bone tool to add nostrils and a Dresden tool to mark a mouth. Shape the remaining pink paste into a dragon's tail. (Use the photograph as a guide.)

2 Knead the black modelling paste until softened. Dust a work surface with icing sugar or cornflour and roll out the paste to 2mm/$\frac{1}{16}$in thick. Cut small triangles to make dragon spikes, as well as a small pear-shaped piece that becomes the crown.

3 Roll two thin sausages to create the 'whiskers' and use edible glue to stick them to the sides of the dragon's pink nose. Roll a pea-sized ball of pink paste, and squash it into an oval disc. Use edible glue to stick it above the nose and then use a ball tool to form two eye sockets.

4 Make two small balls of white paste and place them in the sockets for eyes. Add two smaller balls of black paste to finish the eyes with pupils. Set all the pieces of the dragon aside to dry for at least 24 hours.

5 When the pieces are dry, use edible glue to fix the spikes down the back of the head and the tail, and attach the pear-shaped piece to the top of the head, pointed-end downwards.

TO MAKE THE LOLLIPOPS

1 Knead the red modelling paste until softened. Dust a work surface with icing sugar or cornflour and roll out the paste to 5mm/¼in thick and cut out a 5cm/2in circle. Press a cake pop stick into the back and fix with edible glue. Make a swirl on the front of the lollipop using the Dresden tool.

2 Repeat the process using the green and yellow pastes to make three different-coloured lollipops in total. Leave them all to dry and firm up for at least 24 hours.

TO MAKE THE CAKE

1 Make the vanilla sponge cakes following the recipe instructions on page 8. Once the cakes are cool, level the top of each with a large serrated knife.

2 Using a palette knife, spread about one-third of the buttercream over the top of one cake and sandwich the two cakes together. Secure the stacked cakes to a 28cm/11in cake board or drum with a small amount of buttercream. Spread the remaining buttercream over the top and down the sides of the cake in a smooth, even layer.

3 Knead the white ready-to-roll icing until softened. Dust the work surface with icing sugar or cornflour and roll out the white icing to about 5mm/¼in thick until you have a circle large enough to cover the cake and edges of the board.

4 Using a rolling pin, lift the white icing and drape it over the top of the cake and board. Smooth the icing using a cake smoother, starting on the top then working down the sides and the board to remove any trapped air or creases. Trim the edges of the icing using a small knife, and reserve the offcuts to make flowers. Decorate the edge of the board with a ribbon, using edible glue to secure it into place.

5 To make the lake, on a dusted surface, roll out the brown ready-to-roll icing to about 3mm/⅛in thick, or until it is big

enough to cut out a 20cm/8in circle (you can use a 20cm/8in cake tin for size). Brush the brown circle with edible glue and stick it on the top of the cake.

6 Roll out the yellow icing in the same way, cutting it into two small wavy puddle shapes. You can do this free-form, just ensure that one of the puddles is big enough for Denize to sit in (see picture, page 51). Brush the puddles with edible glue and attach them to the brown lake.

7 Roll out thin sausages of green ready-to-roll icing to make the flower stems and stick them to the sides of the cake with edible glue in groups of two and three (you'll need about 20 stems altogether). Roll out the remaining green icing to 3mm/⅛in thick and cut out small leaves using a 2cm/¾in rose leaf cutter. Pinch together the ends of each leaf to curl them, and attach them to the stems with edible glue.

8 Roll out the leftover white icing to 3mm/⅛in thick and cut out the appropriate number of flowers using a 2.5cm/1in flower cutter. Stick them to the tops of the stems and attach a small ball of red icing to the centre of each flower.

9 Fix the dragon head and tail to the larger of the two yellow puddles, using edible glue. Then, to finish, insert the lollipops into one side of the cake. Denize is ready to meet his favourite Candy Crush Saga fans!

Coconut Wheel Cookies

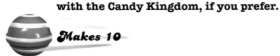

We've given our Coconut Wheel Cookies a tasty chocolate centre, but you could use liquorice wheel sweets for added authenticity with the Candy Kingdom, if you prefer.

Makes 10

- 1 quantity Shortbread Biscuits (see page 11)
- 10 giant chocolate buttons
- 200g/7oz desiccated coconut
- ½ teaspoon pink edible petal dust

Method

1 Make the shortbread biscuit dough following the instructions on page 11, using a 10cm/4in round cutter to cut out the 10 cookies. Bake in the preheated oven for 15-20 minutes until pale golden and leave to cool on a wire rack before decorating.

2 While the cookies are cooling, put the coconut into a sandwich bag with the pink petal dust and shake until the coconut is coloured pink.

3 Brush the top of each cookie with edible glue. Stick a chocolate button in the middle of each cookie, then sprinkle the pink coconut around the buttons to completely coat the top of the cookies. Leave the cookies to set before serving.

Level 2

Easter Bunny Hills Cupcakes

When the Easter Bunny isn't collecting Easter eggs buried in the Easter Bunny Hills, he has stripy carrots to pick and munch on. Each one of these cupcakes is like a little hill of sweetness itself, topped with a cleverly crafted carrot. Divine!

Makes 10

- 1 quantity Vanilla Cupcakes (see page 9)
- ⅛ teaspoon green food-colouring paste
- 1 quantity Buttercream Frosting (see page 12)

- 150g/5½oz white ready-to-roll icing
- 70g/2½oz red ready-to-roll icing
- 70g/2½oz purple ready-to-roll icing
- icing sugar or cornflour, for dusting
- 50g/1¾oz green ready-to-roll icing

Method

1 Make the cupcakes, using bright green cupcake cases, following the instructions on page 9. Once the cupcakes are completely cool, you're ready to start decorating.

2 Stir the green food-colouring paste into the buttercream until it turns the colour of grass. Keep stirring until you get your colour nice and even.

3 Spoon the green buttercream into a piping bag fitted
with a large star nozzle. Using a spiral motion, pipe the
buttercream on the top of each cupcake in a large swirl.

4 To make the carrots, knead the white, red and purple
ready-to-roll icing colours until softened. Dust a work
surface with icing sugar or cornflour and use your hands to
roll each colour into a long sausage, about 5mm/¼in thick.

5 Cut the white icing sausage into two and twist one of the pieces with the red sausage. Repeat with the second white icing sausage and the purple sausage. Cut each red/white and purple/white sausage into 3cm/1¼in-long pieces, so that you have 10 striped pieces altogether.

6 To make the carrot shape, roll each twisted piece between your hands so that one end becomes thinner than the other. Press a cone tool into the thick end to create a little hole. To make a carrot frond, take a pea-sized amount of the green ready-to-roll icing and, using your fingers, roll and shape it into a teardrop shape. Snip the thick end of the teardrop with scissors to create individual leaves, taking care not to snip them off completely. Repeat to make 10 green fronds in total.

7 Dot some edible glue into the hole in each carrot and insert a green icing frond into each hole to complete your carrots. Finally, place a carrot on top of each cupcake to decorate.

Level 2

Candy Cane Cookies

Candy cane stripes pop up all over the Candy Kingdom – they are like the borders of our world. We like to make our Candy Cane Cookies big and chunky – just one of these delicious treats should be enough to fill you up, even when you're really hungry for a Candy-themed snack.

Makes 8

• 1 quantity Gingerbread Biscuits (see page 10)

• 100g/3½oz white Royal Icing (see page 12)
• 100g/3½oz red Royal Icing

Method

1 Preheat the oven, prepare the baking sheets and make the gingerbread biscuit dough following steps 1 and 2 on page 10. Roll out the dough to 5mm/¼in thick on a lightly floured work surface.

2 Using a 15cm/6in-long Candy cane cutter, or the template on page 106, cut out eight canes, re-rolling the dough when necessary.

3 Place the Candy canes on the prepared baking sheets and bake for 12–15 minutes, until just crisp and golden. Leave to cool on a wire rack.

4 Attach a #2 nozzle to a piping bag and spoon in about one third of the white royal icing. Pipe a white border around the edge of each cookie.

To create the cane shape, use a cane-shaped cutter or the template on page 106.

5 Using the same piping bag, pipe seven or eight thin, diagonal lines across the cookies to mark the edges of the stripes (using the photograph on page 62 as a guide). Curve the lines to show the bend of the canes for added authenticity, if you like.

6 Add a little water to the remaining white royal icing until it has the consistency of single cream and spoon it into a second disposable piping bag, this time with no nozzle.

7 Snip the end off the piping bag so you that have a hole about 3mm/⅛in wide. Starting at the top, 'handle' end of the cane, pipe alternate stripes with the white icing, filling the whole area within each marked-out stripe. Take care to keep the icing within the lines so that you'll end up with neat stripes.

8 Loosen the red royal icing with a little water to the consistency of single cream, then spoon it into a new disposable piping bag. Snip the end of the bag, as in step 7, and pipe the red icing into the empty spaces to give an alternate white-and-red striped effect. Leave the icing to dry before eating.

Delicious Drift Igloo Cupcakes

Floating on the icebergs of Delicious Drifts are igloos made not from blocks of ice, but from sweet marshmallows. They are the perfect inspiration for some igloo-shaped cupcakes topped with mounds of buttercream frosting and real marshmallows.

Makes 10

- 1 quantity Vanilla Cupcakes (see page 9)

- 1 quantity Buttercream Frosting (see page 12)
- mini marshmallows, to decorate

Method

1 Make the cupcakes following the instructions on page 9. Pink muffin cases are perfect for your igloo cupcakes. Once the cupcakes are cooked through and golden, leave them to cool on a wire rack.

2 Divide the buttercream evenly between the cupcakes, using a palette knife to spread it into a dome shape on each one.

3 Decorate the cupcakes with mini marshmallows, starting around the lower edge of the buttercream and working round and up to the top of each dome.

Level 3

Lollipop Tree Cake

**There are triple treats in this inspired Candy Kingdom cake –
not only do we have sweet sponge and divine icing, but there
are real Candy lollipops, too! Don't discard the pieces of cake you
cut away as you carve the tree – you'll need to use them to give
the leafy green part its 3D shape.**

Makes one 25cm/10in cake

- 2 quantities 20cm/8in Vanilla
  Sponge Cake batter (see page 8)
- 1 quantity Buttercream Frosting
  (see page 12)

- 250g/9oz green ready-to-roll icing
- icing sugar or cornflour, for
  dusting
- 250g/9oz brown ready-to-roll icing
- 10 mixed fruit lollipops

Method

1 Grease and flour the sides and line the base of a 25cm/10in
cake tin. Preheat the oven and make the cake batter (double
quantity) following step 1 of the instructions on page 8. Pour
the cake batter into the prepared tin and bake it in the oven for
35–40 minutes, or until a skewer inserted into the middle comes
out clean.

2 Remove the cake from the tin and transfer to a wire rack
to cool completely. When the cake is cool, level the top with
a large serrated knife.

3 To form the cake into the shape of a tree, use the tip of a knife to mark out a 5cm/2in-wide trunk in the middle of the bottom half of the cake. When you're happy with the shape you've marked out, use a serrated knife to cut away the cake on either side of the trunk. (Use the photograph on page 69 as a guide.) In the middle towards the top of the trunk, use the knife to cut out a little nick in the sponge – this will form a hollow in the tree trunk once you've covered the cake in icing. Reserve the cut-away pieces of cake.

4 Now shape the top of the tree. Again using a serrated knife, cut away small pieces of sponge so that you create a wavy, rounded shape (see the photograph on page 69). Reserve the cake pieces. Using a palette knife, spread the buttercream over the top of the tree in an even layer. Use the reserved cake offcuts to form mounds that will give the tree a 3D effect once iced (use a little buttercream to mould the offcuts together if you need to).

5 Knead the green ready-to-roll icing until softened. Dust a work surface with icing sugar or cornflour and roll out the icing to 5mm/¼in thick. Cover the top half of the tree with the green icing and mould it into your favourite tree shape, smoothing it gently over the cake mounds as you go.

6 Knead the brown icing until soft, and roll as before on a dusted surface. Place the brown icing over the trunk, cutting away some jagged branch shapes at the top. Tuck the icing into the 'hollow' and around the cake, then trim the edges. Use a Dresden tool to form the bark markings, and to create texture in the green part of the tree. Finally, push the lollipops into the green top. A cake that grows real lollipops? Sweet!

Chocolate Mountains Cake

What a wonderful place for Yeti to fall asleep – among the Chocolate Mountains! This fabulous cake has it all – shards of dark chocolate, rich ganache, and fluffy marshmallows. Divine!

Makes one 15cm/6in cake

- 3 quantities 20cm/8in Chocolate Sponge Cake batter (see page 8)
- 2 quantities Chocolate Ganache (see page 13)
- 200g/7oz plain chocolate, broken into pieces

- blue, pink and white 100s and 1000s, for sprinkling
- 150g/5½oz white chocolate, broken into pieces
- 1 teaspoon pink edible petal dust
- mini marshmallows, to decorate

Method

1 Grease and flour the sides and line the bases of 3 x 15cm/6in cake tins. Preheat the oven and make the cake batter (triple quantity) following step 1 of the instructions on page 8. Divide the batter equally between the three cake tins and bake the cakes for 35–40 minutes, or until a skewer inserted into each centre comes out clean. Remove the cakes from the tins, leave to cool completely, then level the tops with a large serrated knife. Cut each cake in half to make six cakes altogether.

2 Divide one third of the chocolate ganache into five equal portions. Using a palette knife, spread one ganache portion over each of five of the cakes, spreading it out evenly. Sandwich the five cakes together, then top with the sixth cake. Put a small amount of ganache on a 20cm/8in cake board or drum (to act as glue), and then place the layered cake on top.

3 Spread the reserved ganache over the top and down the sides of the cake, as well as over the exposed parts of the cake board, in an even layer. Use a metal side scraper to smooth the edges and give a flat surface.

4 Decorate the edge of the board and the base of the cake with ribbons of your choosing, using edible glue to secure them in place. Chill the cake in the refrigerator for 30 minutes.

5 Meanwhile, make the chocolate shards. Melt the plain chocolate in a microwave, or alternatively place it in a heatproof bowl and set over a pan of simmering water, making sure the bowl doesn't touch the water. Heat gently, stirring, until melted. Remove the bowl from the pan.

6 Spread out the chocolate to about 5mm/¼in thick over a large piece of baking paper. Sprinkle over the differently coloured 100s and 1000s and leave the chocolate to set. Once it has set, using a sharp knife, cut the sprinkled chocolate into five triangles in varying sizes and put to one side.

7 In a clean heatproof bowl, melt the white chocolate, as in step 5, then remove the bowl from the heat and mix in the pink petal dust until the melted chocolate is bright pink.

8 Take the cake out of the fridge and pour the melted pink chocolate over, using a palette knife to spread it out over the top, then let it drip randomly over the sides.

9 While the pink chocolate is still wet, press the chocolate shards into the cake and leave them to set. Finally, scatter over the mini marshmallows to decorate. Delicious!

Swedish Fish Cookies

The Swedish Fish are handy Boosters in Candy Crush Saga
because they love to consume the clear Jelly, improving your
chances of clearing the level. We think such mighty comrades
of the Candy Kingdom deserve their very own cookie friends.
You'll need a Dresden tool to create the detail in the icing, giving
each of the colourful fish its scales and the markings on its fins.
You can decorate either side of the fish-shaped cookies, so that
the results look like they're swimming in all directions. Tasty!

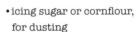

Makes 9

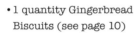

- 1 quantity Gingerbread
  Biscuits (see page 10)
- 100g/3½oz red ready-to-roll
  icing

- icing sugar or cornflour,
  for dusting
- 100g/3½oz green ready-to-roll
  icing
- 100g/3½oz blue ready-to-roll
  icing

Method

1 Make the gingerbread biscuit dough following the
   instructions in steps 1 and 2 on page 10. Roll out the dough
to 5mm/¼in thick on a lightly floured work surface. Using a
12cm/4½in fish-shaped cutter, or the template on page 109,
cut out nine cookies, re-rolling the dough when necessary.

Place the fish on the prepared baking sheets and bake for
12–15 minutes until just crisp and golden. Leave to cool on
a wire rack before decorating.

Once cool, knead the red ready-to-roll icing until softened.
Dust the work surface with icing sugar or cornflour and roll
out the red icing to 3mm/⅛in thick. Cut out three fishes using
the fish-shaped cutter or template.

Brush the biscuits with edible glue and stick the red icing
onto the biscuits. While the icing is still soft, use a Dresden
tool to mark each fish with a dorsal fin, a tail and a head (with a
dot for the eye and little indent for the mouth),
then mark in the scales over the fish body (use
the photograph on page 77 as a guide).

Repeat steps 3 and 4 with the green and
then the blue ready-to-roll icing and the remaining
gingerbread fish. Delicious!

To create the fish use
a fish-shaped cutter
or the template on
page 109.

Target: 9000

Moves: 3

Score: 24442

Liquorice Lock & Blocker Squares

Liquorice Locks and Liquorice Blockers might prove a gameplay challenge, but life's sweet when it comes to eating them!

Makes 4

- 1 quantity 20cm Vanilla Sponge Cake batter (see page 8)
- ⅓ quantity Buttercream Frosting (see page 12)
- liquorice laces, to decorate
- 10g/¼oz grey ready-to-roll icing

Method

1 Grease and flour a 15cm/6in square cake tin. Preheat the oven and make the cake batter according to step 1 on page 8. Pour the batter into the tin and bake for 35–40 minutes, or until a skewer inserted into the centre comes out clean. Remove the cake from the tin, cool completely, then level the top with a large serrated knife. Cut the cake into quarters.

2 Using a palette knife, spread the buttercream over the top of each cake. Decorate two cakes with the liquorice laces in a 'lock' pattern (see photograph, top left); and the remaining cakes using the laces in a spiral, finishing with a pea-sized ball of grey ready-to-roll icing in the middle (top right).

Colour Bomb Cake Pops

These cake pops dipped in chocolate and covered in sprinkles to look like Colour Bombs are divine! You can use vanilla or chocolate sponge for the insides, but we like chocolate best.

Makes 8

- 200g/7oz cake offcuts (vanilla or chocolate)
- 50g/1¾oz Buttercream Frosting (see page 12), softened

- 200g/7oz plain chocolate, broken into pieces
- multi-coloured sprinkles, to decorate

Method

1 Line a baking sheet with baking paper. Blitz the cake offcuts in a food processor until you have fine crumbs. Tip the cake crumbs into a mixing bowl, then mix in the softened buttercream, until fully combined.

2 Using your hands, roll the mixture into eight balls, each about the size of a large walnut. Place the balls on the prepared baking sheet and refrigerate for 30 minutes to firm up.

3 To make the chocolate coating, melt the chocolate in a microwave, or place it in a heatproof bowl and set over a pan of simmering water, making sure the bottom of the bowl doesn't touch the water. Heat gently, stirring the chocolate occasionally, until melted. Remove the bowl from the pan.

4 Remove the cake balls from the fridge. Dip the end of a cake-pop stick into the melted chocolate, then push it into a cake ball. Repeat for all the balls. Return the cake pops to the fridge for about 15 minutes, or until the sticks are secure.

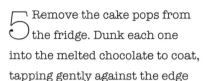

Tiffi's Tip
Cake offcuts will keep in a sandwich bag in the freezer for up to a month.

5 Remove the cake pops from the fridge. Dunk each one into the melted chocolate to coat, tapping gently against the edge of the bowl to remove any excess chocolate. Place the cake pops back onto the baking sheet (or push the sticks into an empty egg box or a polystyrene block, to keep them upright). Leave in a cool place, but not in the fridge, until the chocolate sets.

6 Once set, dip each cake pop for a second time in the melted chocolate (you may need to reheat it briefly) and immediately scatter the sprinkles over. Leave to set.

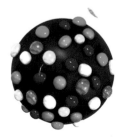

Level 3

Bubblegum Troll Cake

Over the Easter Bunny Hills, lurking under Bubblegum Bridge, lives the troublesome Bubblegum Troll – mischievous and helpful in equal measure. This 3D cake has the happy Bubblegum Troll waving his arms towards you!

Makes one 15cm/6in cake

- 300g/10½oz pink modelling paste
- dried spaghetti
- 2 quantities 23cm/9in Vanilla Sponge Cake batter (see page 8)
- 100g/3½oz white ready-to-roll icing
- icing sugar or cornflour, for dusting
- 1½ quantities Buttercream Frosting (see page 12)
- 750g/1lb 10oz pink ready-to-roll icing
- 10g/¼oz black ready-to-roll icing

Method

FOR THE TROLL'S CURL AND ARMS

1 First, make the troll's curly wisp of hair and his arms, as these will need at least 24 hours to dry and firm up. To make the hair, roll out a thin sausage of pink modelling paste a bit thicker than a strand of spaghetti and 10cm/4in long. Push a piece of spaghetti half way into the sausage, leaving about 5cm/2in poking out of one end. Curl the other end of the paste and leave to dry on a piece of baking paper for at least 24 hours.

2 To make the arms, halve the remaining pink modelling paste. Roll each piece into a thick sausage shape, about 15cm/6in long and slightly thicker at one end. Slightly flatten the thinner end to create a hand and make three snips with scissors to create four fingers.

3 Push a strand of spaghetti into the thick end of each arm and then place the arms on the piece of baking paper with the hair curl and leave to dry for at least 24 hours.

FOR THE CAKE

1 Grease and flour the sides and line the base of 4 x 15cm/6in cake tins. Preheat the oven and make the cake batter (double quantity) following step 1 on page 8. Pour equal amounts of batter into each tin and bake the cakes for 35–40 minutes, or until a skewer inserted into the middle comes out clean. Remove the cakes from the tins, cool completely, then level the top of each cake with a large serrated knife.

2 Meanwhile, lightly brush a 23cm/9in cake board or drum with water. Knead the white ready-to-roll icing until softened. Dust the work surface with icing sugar or cornflour and roll out the icing to a circle about 5mm/¼in thick and large enough to cover the cake board.

3 Using a rolling pin, lay the white icing carefully over the board, then smooth with a cake smoother, and trim the edges with a small knife, reserving any offcuts. Set aside.

4 Halve the buttercream and divide one half into three. Using a palette knife, spread one third over the top of one of the cakes, then repeat with the remaining two thirds and two further cakes. Place the cakes one on top of the other to sandwich them together. Top the stack with the fourth cake.

5 Using a serrated knife, carve the cake into a dome shape, then cover the dome in the remaining buttercream.

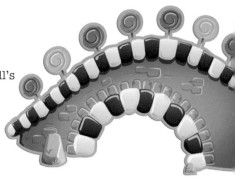

6 To form the outline of the troll's mouth, roll some of the pink ready-to-roll icing into a long sausage and use edible glue to stick it to the cake in the shape of an open mouth.

7 Knead the remaining pink icing until softened. Dust a work surface with icing sugar or cornflour and roll out the icing to about 5mm/¼in thick and so that it is a large enough circle (about 33cm/13in diameter) to cover the entire cake.

8 Brush the whole cake, including the outline of the mouth, with water. Place the pink icing circle over the top of the cake and let it drape loosely. Smooth the icing over the head and face, but leave it hanging at the bottom, then trim the bottom edge using a small knife. Carefully transfer the cake to the cake board.

9 Halve the black icing and roll it in your hands into two small balls for the troll's eyes. Fix them to the cake with edible glue.

10 Roll four small balls of the remaining white ready-to-roll icing, two slightly larger than the others, and attach one larger and one smaller ball to each eye with the glue to create the troll's twinkling pupils.

11 Roll out the remaining white icing until it is about 3mm/⅛in thick. Use a wheel tool to cut out the complete shape of the troll's teeth. Stick the white shape inside the mouth outline. Use a Dresden tool to mark the individual teeth. (Use the photograph on page 87 to help you.)

12 Put a dot of edible glue on the top of the troll's head where the curl of hair will go and gently push the spaghetti supporting the curl into the cake. Attach the arms in the same way, placing a dot of glue on each side of the troll and gently pressing the spaghetti supporting the arms into the cake. Your Bubblegum Troll is ready, waving his arms to grab your attention!

Caramel Cove Cupcakes

These fudge-topped cupcakes inspired by the sweet toffiness of Caramel Cove are simple to make and delicious to eat!

Makes 10

- 1 quantity Vanilla Cupcakes (see page 9)
- 1 quantity Buttercream Frosting (see page 12)
- fudge or toffee pieces, to decorate
- toffee syrup, to decorate

Method

1 Make the cupcakes following the instructions on page 9, this time using brown cupcake cases. Leave the cakes to cool on a wire rack before decorating.

2 Spoon the buttercream into a piping bag fitted with a large star nozzle. Pipe the buttercream, using a spiral motion, on the top of each cupcake in a large swirl. Spoon a little toffee syrup over each cupcake, then top with fudge or toffee pieces. Tiki, the Caramel Chieftain, approves!

Level 3

Pastille Pyramid Cake

Layers of vanilla sponge, wrapped in buttercream and decorated with multi-coloured pastille Candies, make this real-life version of the Pastille Pyramid impossible to resist. Keep the offcuts as you carve the cake – you'll need them to build the pyramid to its uppermost point.

Makes one 15cm/6in cake

- 2 quantities 20cm/8in Vanilla Sponge Cake batter (see page 8)
- 200g/7oz ivory ready-to-roll icing
- icing sugar or cornflour, for dusting
- ¾ quantity Buttercream Frosting (see page 12)
- 600g/1lb 5oz American hard gums or sugar-coated pastilles

Method

1 Grease and flour the sides and line the base of 2 x 15cm/6in square cake tins. Preheat the oven and make the cake batter (double quantity) following step 1 on page 8. Divide the batter equally between the two tins and bake the cakes for 35–40 minutes, or until a skewer inserted into the centre comes out clean. Remove the cakes from the tins, cool completely, then level the tops with a large serrated knife.

Tiffi's Tip #1

When placing the sweets, start at the bottom and work upwards, completing one row on all four sides before moving up to the next row. It can be handy to put the cake on a Lazy Susan, if you have one, so that you can turn it easily!

$\mathcal{2}$ While the cakes are baking, lightly brush a 20cm/8in square cake board or drum with water. Knead the ivory ready-to-roll icing until softened. Dust a work surface with icing sugar or cornflour and roll out the ivory icing to a square about 5mm/¼in thick and large enough to cover the cake board.

$\mathcal{3}$ Place the rolled ivory icing over the board, smoothing it out with a cake smoother, and trimming the edges with a small knife to neaten. Set aside.

4 Using a palette knife, spread about one third of the buttercream over the top of one cake and place the second cake on top to sandwich the two cakes together.

5 Using a serrated knife, carefully slice the stacked cake so that you begin to form the shape of the pyramid. Use the offcuts to help create the shape and to build up the top of the pyramid as necessary into a point (use a little buttercream to stick any pieces together if you need to). Spread a small amount of buttercream (as a glue) over the centre of the cake board and carefully transfer the whole cake to the board.

6 Using a palette knife, spread the remaining buttercream over the cake in a smooth, even layer, taking care with the parts of the pyramid you've built up using offcuts. While the buttercream is still soft, place the American hard gums or pastilles in rows up the sides of the cake to decorate.

Tiffi's Tip #2
When you decorate, try to ensure no two sweets of the same colour are next to each other in a row.

Gameboard Cake

We couldn't have a Candy Crush Cakes & Bakes book without a cake made to look like a gameboard. This one takes patience and some skill, but it's so much fun it's worth it (a bit like Candy Crush Saga itself!). You can arrange your Candies into any screen formation you like, and if you're feeling confident you could even add some mini Colour Bomb Cake Pops (see page 82) to the board as well.

Makes one 20cm/8in cake

- 2 quantities 23cm/9in Vanilla Sponge Cake batter (see page 8)
- 1½ quantities Buttercream Frosting (see page 12)
- 750g/1lb 10oz white ready-to-roll icing
- icing sugar or cornflour, for dusting

- 100g/3½oz navy blue ready-to-roll icing
- 20g/¾oz red ready-to-roll icing
- 20g/¾oz orange ready-to-roll icing
- 20g/¾oz yellow ready-to-roll icing
- 20g/¾oz green ready-to-roll icing
- 20g/¾oz royal blue ready-to-roll icing
- 20g/¾oz purple ready-to-roll icing

Method

1 Grease and flour the sides and line the bases of 2 x 20cm/8in square cake tins. Preheat the oven and make the cake batter (double quantity) following step 1 on page 8. Divide the batter equally between the two tins and bake for 35–40 minutes, or until a skewer inserted into the cakes' centres comes out clean.

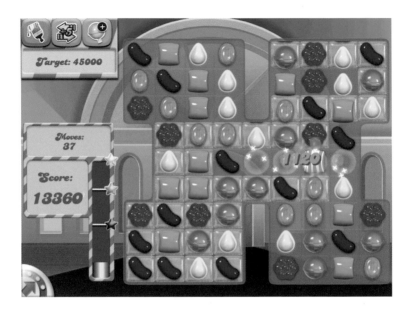

Remove the cakes from the tins, cool completely, then level the top of each cake with a large serrated knife.

2 Using a palette knife, spread a third of the buttercream over the top of one cake and place the other cake on top, sandwiching the two cakes together.

3 Spread the remaining buttercream over the top and down the sides of the stacked cakes in a smooth, even layer.

4 Knead the white ready-to-roll icing until softened. Dust the work surface with icing sugar or cornflour and roll out the white icing into a square about 5mm/¼in thick and large enough to cover the top and sides of the cake.

5 Using a rolling pin, lift the white icing and drape it over the top of the cake. Smooth the icing using a cake smoother, starting on the top, then working down the sides to remove any trapped air or creases. Trim the edges of the icing using a small knife. Decorate the bottom edge of the cake with a ribbon, using a small amount of buttercream to secure it.

6 Knead the navy blue ready-to-roll icing until softened. Dust the work surface with icing sugar or cornflour and roll out the navy blue icing to 5mm/¼in thick. Cut out an 18cm/7in square and mark vertical and horizontal lines, about 2.5cm/1in apart, with a Dresden tool. Cut out and discard each corner square, creating the gameboard grid. Stick the blue gameboard grid to the top of the cake using edible glue.

7 Shape the other colours of ready-to-roll icing into the different core Candies, forming them by hand into red jelly beans, orange lozenges, yellow lemon drops, green gum squares, blue lollipop heads and purple jujube clutters, using the photograph as a guide. Arrange the finished Candies into the grid on top of the cake, attaching them with edible glue. Sweet!

Candy Cake Pops

From jelly beans to lollipop heads, there are a number of different core Candies that the Candy Kingdom just can't do without. What better way to celebrate the essential Candies of gameplay than with Candy-shaped cake pops? You can shape these cake pops by hand, or use a mould if you're on a time limit!

Makes 6

- 150g/5½oz cake offcuts (we like chocolate cake offcuts best)
- 40g/1½oz Buttercream Frosting (see page 12), softened
- 100g/3½oz blue Candy Melts

- 100g/3½oz yellow Candy Melts
- 100g/3½oz red Candy Melts
- 100g/3½oz orange Candy Melts
- 100g/3½oz green Candy Melts
- 100g/3½oz purple Candy Melts

Method

1 Line a baking sheet with baking paper. Blitz the cake offcuts in a food processor until you have fine crumbs. Tip the cake crumbs into a mixing bowl, then mix in the softened buttercream, until fully combined.

2 Using your hands, divide the mixture into six balls, each one about the size of a large walnut. Shape each ball, using your hands or a mould, into a different core Candy. Shape one ball into a jelly bean, one into a lozenge, one into a lemon drop,

Tiffi's Tip
Remember: you can keep any cake offcuts in a sandwich bag in the freezer for 1 month.

one into a gum square, one into a lollipop head and the final ball into the jujube clutter. Use the photograph as a guide to the shape of each Candy. Place each shape onto the prepared baking sheet and chill in the fridge for 30 minutes to firm up.

3 Melt the Candy Melts following the instructions on the packaging. Remove the Candy shapes cake pops from the fridge. Dip the end of a cake-pop stick into the Candy Melts, then push it into a cake pop, matching the colour of the Candy Melt to the colour of the core Candy. Repeat for all the core Candy cake pops. Place the cake pops back on the baking sheet and chill for about a further 15 minutes, or until the sticks are secure.

4 Remove the cake pops from the fridge. Dunk each one into the Candy Melts, again matching the colours, until coated, and tap gently to remove any excess Candy Melt. Place the core Candy cake pops back on the baking sheet, or insert the cake-pop sticks into an empty egg box or a polystyrene block if you have one, to keep the cake pops upright. Chill until the Candy Melt has set.

5 Once the cake pops have set, dip each one for a second time into the Candy Melts, if needed (you may need to reheat the Candy Melt briefly), for a final coat and leave to set again. Glossy!

Templates

These are all the templates you'll need to make the biscuits in the book. The templates are actual size, so all you have to do is copy or trace them onto card, then cut them out so that you can cut round them easily when placed on your biscuit dough. Last of all, on page 111, you'll find the templates for making the icing features for Odus the Owl.

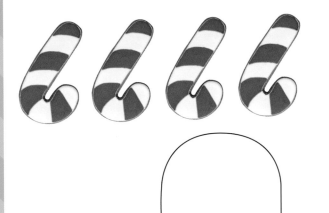

Candy Cane Cookies
see page 62

Star Iced Cookies
see page 16

Lollipop Forest Flower Cookies

see page 42

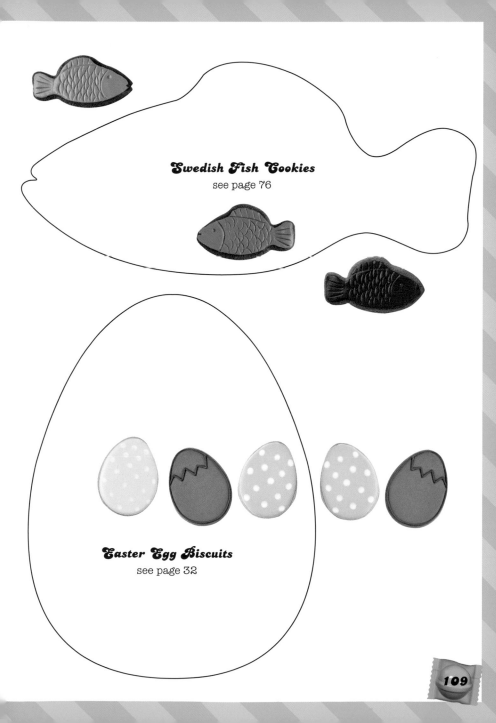

Swedish Fish Cookies
see page 76

Easter Egg Biscuits
see page 32

Gingerbread Girls
see page 22

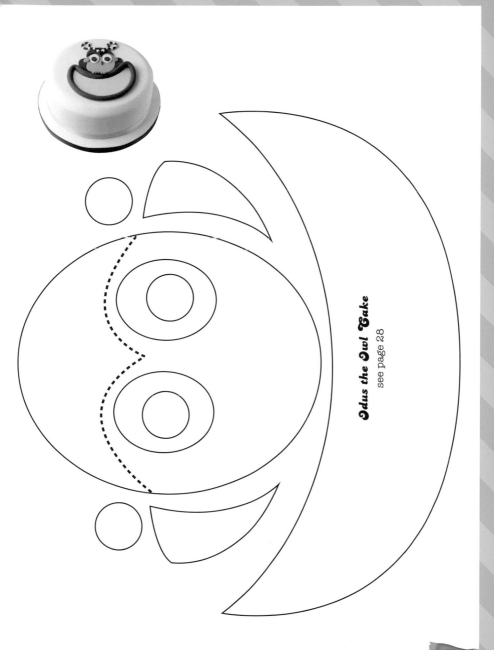

Odus the Owl Cake
see page 28

Acknowledgements

The Publisher would like to thank the team at King, and everyone at Bath Cake Company – Celia Adams, and Zulekha, Sarah, Rebecca and Nicole – for their invaluable help creating this book.

www.bathcakecompany.co.uk